USAF FOR THE 21st CENTURY

USAF FOR THE 21st CENTURY

SUPER WING TOTAL FORCE INTEGRATION

JAMES BENSON AND TONY HOLMES

OSPREY
AEROSPACE

ISBN 1 85532 617 5

Page Design by Paul Kime

Printed in Hong Kong

Title page *The unmistakeable planform of the now-veteran F-15C Eagle as seen from the 'boomer's' window at the rear of a 22nd Air Refueling Squadron (ARS) KC-135R. This machine hails from the 390th Fighter Squadron (FS), the sole fighter-optimised unit within the 366th Wing at Mountain Home. Camouflaged in the now-fashionable 'Mod Eagle' 'soft greys', the jet boasts an AIM-9M acquisition round on the port LAU-114 twin Sidewinder pylon and a Cubic Corporation Air Combat Manoeuvring Instrumentation (ACMI) Pod on the starboard outer rail. The latter acts as an airborne sensor, transmitting the aircraft's altitude, speed, turn and bank, climb and descent, G-loading, weapons status and HUD picture to the Tactical Air Combat Training System (TACTS) computer back at base in real time, via a series of microwave links. Allied with an uncaged and 'growling' Sidewinder head, the two stores combine to give the Eagle pilot as true a sense of actual combat (both during the sortie and in the debrief back at base) as can be achieved when tackling an 'adversary' in air combat without actually 'loosing off' a round*

For a catalogue of all books published by Osprey Aerospace please write to:

**The Marketing Department, Osprey Aerospace/Reed Books,
2nd Floor, Unit 6, Citadel Place, Spring Gardens, Tinworth Street,
Vauxhall, London SE11 5EH**

All US military establishments the world over have a main-gate sign which resembles a 'coming attractions' billboard at a drive-in! 'Gunfighters' is the official nickname of the 366th Wing, as this photograph clearly attests to

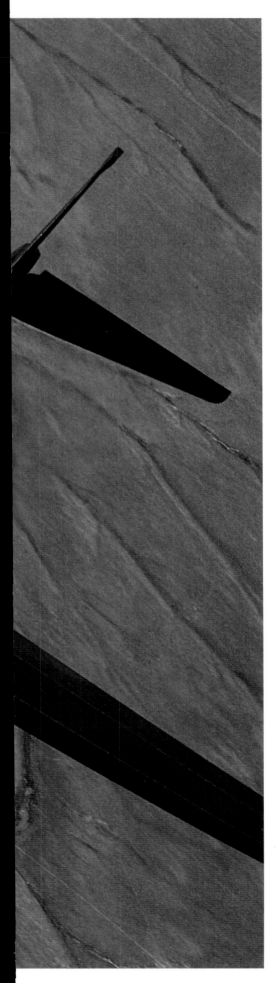

CONTENTS

Left *Although far newer than the veteran B-52Gs they replaced in early 1994 within the 34th BS, the B-1B 'Bones' offer mission planners at the 366th far fewer options when it comes to formulating profiles for their deployment in combat. Having lost the SIOP (Single Integrated Operating Plan) role which, in a time of global conflict, would have seen dozens of B-1Bs racing towards the former Soviet Union independently of one another, toting a belly load of nuclear-tipped Air-Launched Cruise Missiles (ALCMs), the 'Bone' has been denuded of its offensive capability. Indeed, the range of ordnance it is presently cleared to carry is far less extensive than that available to an F-16C. In fact, as of early 1996 only the Mk 82 AIR 500-lb 'dumb' bomb is cleared for use by the B-1B, the aircraft typically carrying 56 rounds in two Conventional Weapon Modules fitted in the jet's middle and aft bomb bays in place of the rotary launchers for the ALCMs*

INTRODUCTION

A model force structure for the 21st century, or just a legacy of the *Desert Storm* experience, the composite, or 'super', wing has both its advocates and its critics in the modern US Air Force. The latter have argued that the 366th Wing is essentially a 'jack of all trades, master of none' organisation that is too small to cope with a Gulf War type situation, but too large to effectively integrate into an all-encompassing battle plan should the USAF become embroiled in a full-scale conflict.

Its instigator, former USAF Chief of Staff Gen Merrill A 'Tony' McPeak, developed the composite wing just as 'his' air force was undergoing the greatest reorganisation in its history. Born alongside Air Combat Command, the 366th Wing has been structured to function as an effective rapid reaction force in both war and peace, on a global basis. It brings together a total of 58 aircraft split between six units, all of which share a common base and integrated command, control, communications and intelligence. F-16 'drivers' originally brief alongside B-1B crews, and F-15C pilots discuss mission tactics with F-15E 'jocks'. Furthermore, offensive assets can rely on dedicated AWACS, ECM support and tankers — in essence, all that is required to prosecute a standard Gulf War-style wing strike is on call at Mountain Home AFB, in Idaho.

The command structure has also been overhauled to reflect changes out on the ramp, with the 366th commander having total autonomy over the deployment of his jets. All mission air tasking orders (ATOs) are generated and duly executed within the wing, principally because the *raison d'être* of the 366th is to go into action as an intervention wing at the start of any possible conflict.

To help facilitate this rapid reaction tasking, a commonality of equipment was strictly adhered to by USAF planners, as the supply chain may be a little stretched at the start of a deployment. To this end, two-thirds of the aircraft in the wing are powered by a common engine, thus reducing the quantity of spares needed to support a det overseas.

The 366th was activated at the former F-111 base at Mountain Home on 1 June 1992, although it didn't acquire its full complement of aircraft until some months later. By 1993 the 366th was considered mature enough to undertake its first exercise in the shape of *Green Flag 93-3* at Nellis, followed soon after by a cross-country wing-strength det to Volk Field, in Wisconsin. Both presented different challenges to the new composite structure, the bulk of which were considered to have been dealt with satisfactorily.

In 1994 the B-52Gs were retired by the USAF, with the Mountain Home aircraft actually being the last sent to Davis-Monthan. The seven 'Buffs' assigned to the 366th had remained at Castle AFB, California, throughout their spell with the wing in order to reduce downtime due to spares shortages, and a similar arrangement was implemented with the arrival of B-1B — the latter are based at Ellsworth, South Dakota.

Although the 'Buffs' had been a part of the Mountain Home set up for less than two years, the versatility they offered mission planners had been fully exploited, and the type's retirement significantly

Above *Looking resplendent in their recently-applied 'MO' tailcodes and distinctive squadron fin flashes, seven of the 389th FS's 24 Fighting Falcons sit idling on the ramp at Mountain Home prior to performing a routine bombing exercise over the range at nearby Saylor Creek – note the 25-lb BDU-33 'blue bombs' fitted to the Triple Ejector Racks (TERs) on each of the jets. This ubiquitous device simulates the ballistics of the Mk 82 Snake Eye (SE) 500-lb retarded weapon, which is a staple 'dumb' bomb in Air Combat Command (ACC). 'BDU' stands for Bomb Dummy Unit, this acronym being applied to the training weapon by the USAF following its adoption after several years' service with the US Navy as the Mk 76. Literally thousands of these inexpensive bombs are dropped on numerous ranges across America every year, thus allowing 'mud movers' in all branches of the US military to hone their weapons delivery skills at a fraction of the cost incurred when using pukka ordnance*

reduced the 366th's effectiveness. Indeed, this has still to be fully restored as this book went to press due to the B-1B's presently restricted weapons suite. The imminent double retirement of the specialised F-4G and EF-111A aircraft has also hurt the wing (and the air force in general), although the void left has been partially filled by the recent arrival of

HARM missile-capable F-16Cs at Mountain Home.

Another asset proving difficult to integrate into daily mission taskings is the E-3 Sentry due to escalating overseas commitments for the USAF's badly-stretched AWACS force.

Despite these recent setbacks, the 366th Wing continues to build on its solid, if unspectacular, record as a unique part of the USAF's order of battle in the late 1990s. Exercise results have not been as good as was originally hoped for, and a lack of coffers in the defence budget has restricted the wing deploying overseas to test its mettle in a truly austere environment. However, new aircraft like the F-16C Block 52 and the B-1B have been issued to the 366th over the past two years, thus showing that the senior brass in the Pentagon still have faith in the concept.

Perhaps the greatest test of Gen 'Tony' McPeak's 'super wing' lay not in its theoretical performance over the battlefield of some far-flung flashpoint on the other side of the globe, but in its ability to survive the swingeing defence cuts currently in vogue in the Pentagon. As of the publication of this volume in the summer of 1996 – the first dedicated solely to the 366th Wing – its future is still very much in the balance . . .

CHAPTER ONE

390th FIGHTER SQUADRON

Left *The Crew Chief personally ensures that all the finishing touches are completed on 'his' jet prior to a mission being flown, and if that means giving the huge canopy on the Eagle a final polish with a lint-free cloth, then so be it. One of the jet's most distinctive features, the one-piece canopy is formed from giant sheets of acrylic plastic, which give the pilot a virtually unobstructed view through 360° when airborne. Small touches like the thorough polishing of a fighter's transparencies can pay off in the long run, as the last thing a pilot wants when on the cusp of a high-speed merge is for his vision to be distracted by smudges and marks on the windscreen and canopy whilst 'eyes' out, looking for his adversary*

Above Although flying the sleek Eagle, the 390th FS retains the 'Wild Boars' motif from its F-111/EF-111 days when the 366th was a Tactical Fighter Wing. Although a relative newcomer to the F-15C when compared with other ACC units, the 390th nevertheless has a proud history 'in fighters' that stretches back to its activation in June 1943 as one of three units in the all-new 366th Fighter Group (FG). Equipped with the P-47 Thunderbolt, the 390th went with its parent unit to Britain at the end of that year as part of the massive reinforcement of the Ninth Air Force. Flying the Thunderbolt throughout its 18 months in combat, the 390th topped the kill tally list for the 366th with 37.5 victories. It also produced the group's only ace, Capt Mel Paisley, who downed five German aircraft in the last six months of the war in Europe

Right Whilst the canopy is rendered spotless the aircraft's ordnance is also given a thorough 'once over'. The Remove Before Flight and T-Key fluorescent orange flags can be seen dangling below the Eagle, which is parked on a quiet Volk Field, Wisconsin, flightline during a Wing deployment. Like most USAF F-15Cs, this machine is fitted with a near-obligatory 600-US gal centreline tank, which is fully G-rated.

The 390th FS was inactivated along with the 366th FG soon after hostilities ceased in Europe, and remained dormant until hastily reformed as a fighter-bomber squadron towards the end of the Korean War in January 1953 at Alexandria AFB, Louisiana

Above *The Eagle has a voracious appetite for JP-4, so the base refuelling tankers are constantly kept busy shuttling to and from the flightline between sorties. Aside from the main fuel hose connecting the Mack with the aircraft, two anti-static charge lines are also attached to the tanker, thus averting the chance of fuel igniting in the jet's tank through kinetic discharge as they fill up.*

Equipped with decidedly obsolescent F-51Ds hastily retrieved from Air National Guard (ANG) units across the US, the squadron was again part of the 366th, which had been redesignated an FBW. The Mustangs soon gave way firstly to F-86s and then F-84Fs, which were in turn replaced by F-100Ds in 1957. The 366th FBG changed into a TFW soon after the arrival of Super Sabres, but was inactivated once again in 1959

Below A pre-flight inspection takes both the ground and aircrew all over the jet prior to the 'wick(s) being lit'. Kitted out in a G-suit and life-preserver vastly reduces the pilot's agility, so more comfortably attired airmen are assigned the task of gingerly clambering over the spine of the Eagle to check that its twin rudders have unrestricted movement once activated by their respective Ronson rotary hydraulic motors. The silver boot covers worn by all groundcrew when walking on fast jets can just be seen on the feet of this individual. 86-181 is the sole dual-seat F-15D assigned to the 390th FS, and like all Eagle 'fighters' at Mountain Home, formerly served with the 33rd FW at Eglin, in Florida.

Turning the clock back over three decades, the 366th TFW was reformed as a result of increased Cold War tension at Chaumont AB, in France, in May 1962, although such was the shortage in frontline equipment at the time that its three squadrons (including the 390th TFS) had to make do with ex-ANG F-84Fs. It returned to the US in July of the following year, being sent to Hollomon AFB, New Mexico, where it flew a mixed force of venerable F-84Fs alongside more youthful F-100Ds. Examples of the then new F-4C were issued to the 366th just prior to it moving to Phan Rang AB, in South Vietnam, in March 1966. What followed was six years of combat over the jungles of South-East Asia, with the 366th pulling one of the longest tours of duty experienced by any frontline USAF wing. Whilst in-theatre, the wing had external SUU-16 or -23 gun pods fitted to its Phantom IIs to give its crews added self-protection should they be bounced by MiGs 'north of the border'. From this fitment was derived the 366th's nickname, 'Gunfighters'

Above *The starboard Ronson rotary actuator is regularly checked for torsional tightness after a hectic series of short, but high-G intensive, ACM 'hops' like those flown by the 390th FS during their det to Volk Field. The incredible forces exerted on the Eagle's twin fins during a 'fur ball fight' with an agile aggressor like the F-16 can have a detrimental affect on the rudders' tautness over a period of time. Having donned his boot 'bags', this airman has mounted the jet and is getting to grips with the actuator*

Right *Like 86-161, this F-15C was also a former Eglin resident with the 33rd TFW. Designated the wing commander's jet, it has 366th titling on its fins (also note the GUNFIGHTERS legend and revolver) and the obligatory drop-shadow tailcodes as worn on all ACC 'boss birds'. The bullet fairing atop the port fin contains the forward and aft jammers of the Northrop Grumman AN/ALQ-135C ICS (Internal Countermeasures Set), which can handle both pulse and continuous wave radar emissions. This fully automated system can be left by the pilot to modify its signal to counter any changes in radar frequency employed by the hostile emitter. A further circular polarised jammer (again part of the AN/ALQ-135C system) is fitted in a rounded tip on the starboard tailboom of the F-15C.*

Scabbed onto the fin trailing edge between the bullet fairing and the port anti-collision light is a Loral ALR-56 Radar Warning Receiver (RWR) spiral-form radome, just one of four (plus an underside blade aerial) fitted to the F-15 to give the jet all-round threat coverage. This system can search out hostile signals, classify them, and then pinpoint their source of origin all in the time it has taken to read this sentence. Once the threat has been analysed, the information is passed to the AN/ALQ-135, which then jams the emitter. Both systems are an integral part of the Tactical Electronic Warfare System (TEWS), the 'brain' of which is a series of electonic boxes which fit snugly into the space immediately behind the pilot. Only USAF F-15s (all versions) have TEWS, the system being developed concurrently with the aircraft itself in the early 1970s

Below With the previous generations of USAF jet fighters, performing an engine change meant that the aircraft disappeared into the corner of a hangar for days on end, as squadron engineers slowly reduced the airframe to components to extricate the offending powerplant. With the F-15, an engine can be slid out of the rear fuselage and onto a railed cradle in just 20 minutes if need be. Its replacement Pratt & Whitney F100-PW-220 unit also makes use of a similar apparatus, as shown here at Volk Field. Another unique feature of the Eagle is that its powerplants are inter-changeable: this freshly unwrapped F100 could be slotted into either engine bay

Above A wealth of airframe detail can be picked out in this rear view of an Eagle being 'uncovered' at the start of another day's flying. Perhaps the most striking design feature of the McDonnell Douglas fighter when observed from this angle is the close proximity of its twin F100 engines. This layout was chosen primarily to avoid asymmetric thrust problems, but the flipside of this arrangement is that both engines can be affected should one catch fire. To reduce the chances of this occurring, the manufacturers have fitted a titanium firewall between the two engines, which seems to have done the trick on the few occasions an F100 has 'detonated' in flight

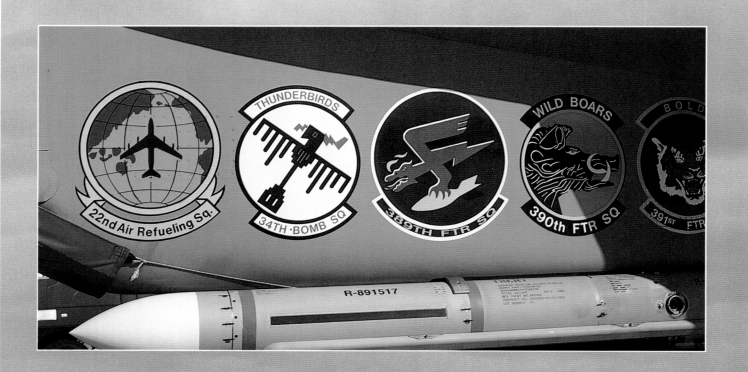

Left Three 'Mod Eagle' grey and three TAC grey F-15s head the line up at Volk Field, with a further six Strike Eagles completing the det force. All the 390th machines in this shot came from the same St Louis production batch built in 1987/88, and issued to the 33rd TFW's 59th TFS, nicknamed 'Golden Pride'. Their arrival in Florida completed the wing's transition from A-models to the very first Multi-Staged Improvement Program (MSIP) F-15Cs then in USAF service. With the formation of the 366th Wing in 1992, the re-rolled 390th FS was equipped exclusively with 20 aircraft from the 'Golden Pride', which in turn received replacements from the deac-tivated 525th FS, formerly with the 36th FW at Bitburg in Germany

Inset Few USAF F-15s wear BS and ARS badges on their intakes, but perhaps this simple array of unit decals on the wing commander's Eagle accu-rately sums up the 'total force' concept of the 366th. Below the unit crests is an inert AIM-7M Sparrow round.

Returning briefly to the Vietnam war, after playing a key role in the Linebacker strikes of May 1972, the 366th was given orders to return to the US and reform on the new F-111F at Mountain Home – here it has remained ever since, although the 390th exchanged its F-models for older F-111As July 1977, followed by re-equipment with EF-111As five years later. It retained its 'Spark Varks' until receiving two-dozen F-15Cs in September 1992

Left All trussed up in his Nomex flying suit, 'speed jeans' (g-suit), parachute harness and survival vest, Lt Col Jim Moschgat flicks through the Form 781 following the completion of his clockwise walkaround of the jet. This weighty volume has the aircraft's entire service history in it, complete with current 'write ups' denoting minor problems with the jet that haven't yet been rectified, but that are equally too minor to warrant grounding the fighter. Once satisfied that his steed is truly airworthy, Moschgat will carefully scale the jet's integral boarding ladder and strap himself in

Inset Storeless, bar the mandatory centreline tank and a Sidewinder acquisition round, F-15C 86-161 is guided along the taxyway with its navigation and collision lights ablaze by Col Jerry Callen, Vice-Commander of the 366th. Most ground taxying to and from the runway is restricted to speeds of 15 to 20 mph, with the pilot steering the jet through rudder pedal inputs – they are connected to the nosewheel at low speeds. A yellow centreline is painted on all USAF taxyways as an aid to pilots, who try to stick to this like glue. Indeed, a sure sign of an inexperienced pilot is a jet that tends to deviate from this route marker

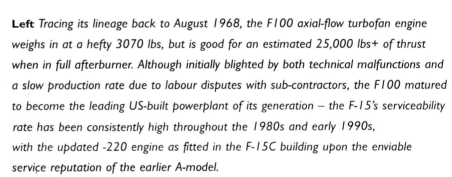

Left *Tracing its lineage back to August 1968, the F100 axial-flow turbofan engine weighs in at a hefty 3070 lbs, but is good for an estimated 25,000 lbs+ of thrust when in full afterburner. Although initially blighted by both technical malfunctions and a slow production rate due to labour disputes with sub-contractors, the F100 matured to become the leading US-built powerplant of its generation – the F-15's serviceability rate has been consistently high throughout the 1980s and early 1990s, with the updated -220 engine as fitted in the F-15C building upon the enviable service reputation of the earlier A-model.*

When viewed from the rear, the Eagle's twin afterburner nozzles tend to dominate, and a closer inspection of the latter reveals a complex system of push rods, sliding runners and titanium plating, discoloured through its exposure to incredible levels of heat. When originally built, the F-15A had its nozzle 'mechanicals' covered with augmentor sealing flaps, known as 'turkey feathers' to 'Eagle keepers'. In theory they were supposed to both protect the complex myriad of moving parts and streamline airflow around the rear end of the jet. The system had worked fine on the prototype and pre-production aircraft, but once in everyday service the consistently intense levels of heat associated with the afterburning engines caused the flaps to warp, thus stopping them from meshing properly when the nozzles 'dilated'. As a result of these technical problems, maintenance of the flaps proved both costly and time-consuming, and they were duly removed

Above *Heat haze bathes the photographer as a four-ship of F-15Cs taxies away from the Volk Field flightline towards the runway. The pure fighter-optimised Eagle is a lithe beast with a very thin cross-section, as this low angle clearly shows*

Left *Having only recently arrived to assume command at Mountain Home from his former position as Wing Commander of the 1st TFW at Langley AFB, Virginia, Gen David J 'Marshal' McCloud eases 'his' jet in behind the KC-135R. The impressive row of unit badges on the intake and drop-shadow tail codes on the fin clash markedly with the matt shades of the 'Mod Eagle' scheme. Once McCloud is happy that he has positioned the jet correctly, he will retract the refuelling receptacle cover on the bulbous port wing shoulder and wait for the boom to be lowered by the tanker*
(Photo by Randy Jolly)

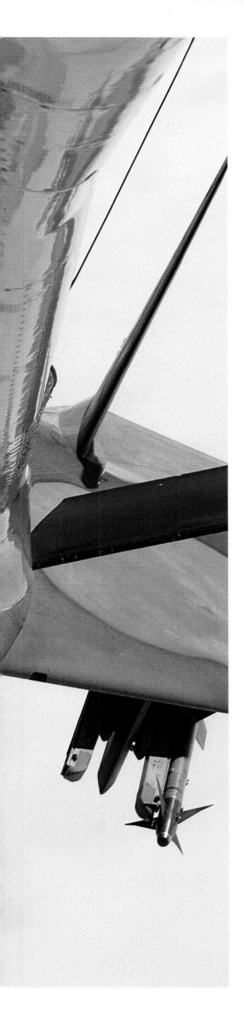

Left The tanker and its customer usually rendezvous at an altitude of between 20,000 and 25,000 ft, with both jets maintaining a cruising speed of 320 kts once the boom has been deployed. The fighter arrives on the tanker's right wing and then awaits the signal from the boom operator to pull in 50 ft astern of the KC-135. Once trailing the tanker, the pilot then slowly closes on the extended boom, his distance to run being relayed to him over the radio by the boomer. To assist the former in positioning the Eagle, a yellow band is painted on the belly of the tanker and Pilot Direction Indicators (PDIs), in the form of a traffic light arrangement, offer further visual cues as to the receiver's height.

Once boom and receptacle are just inches apart, and both jets are flying a smooth oval track pattern, the pilot will call 'on the Apple', which refers to the orange ball painted on the boom itself being in perfect alignment with the receptacle. The boomer uses this signal as an indicator to extend the fuel pipe the last few inches into the receptacle, using hydraulic pressure to force entry. With both jets now unified, the co-pilot of the tanker activates the fuel flow and the transfer commences. One of the great advantages of the flying boom method of aerial refuelling as opposed to probe and drogue operations is that a tanker can transfer greater quantities of fuel to a receiving jet thanks to an increased flow rate. This allows a fighter to spend more time out on patrol rather than hooked up to a tanker.

The F-15 can receive 2000 to 2500 lbs of JP-4 per minute, which usually means that an average refuelling should take between five and ten minutes. This time can obviously be longer if the jet is in transit with external tanks or Conformal Fuel Tanks (CFTs – formerly known as FAST packs) fitted. Once the Eagle's thirst has been quenched the fuel flow is shut off and the boom retracted, ready for the next customer. The fast jet pilot will usually drop slightly back behind the tanker, before accelerating into a formating position off the KC-135's port wing tip and then returning to his patrol line

Above *Second only to the Wing Commander's aircraft in the F-15C 'pecking order' at Mountain Home is the 'boss bird' of the squadron CO. As befits his rank, the 390th's 'senior pilot' flies a spotless jet which is a perfect advert for the unit's maintenance section. Armed with four inert AIM-9Ms, the jet's delicately shaded 'Mod Eagle' scheme stands out well against the snowy ground below. A lot of paint has to be used to cover the F-15's 608 sq ft of wing area – with a flying surface of that dimension it is little wonder that Eagle adversaries soon dubbed the jet the 'supersonic tennis court'*

Below *Whilst his flight leader tops off his tanks in 86-144, the pilot of 86-162 holds formation off to starboard until it his turn to 'fly the boom'. Both jets are equipped with Sparrow acquisition rounds and centreline tanks. Throughout its time on station, the KC-135R will orbit at a constant height and velocity in a gentle oval, or racetrack, pattern in the briefed air refuelling area (ARA)*

Above *Few photographs could better illustrate the subtle tonal differences between the old and new air superiority greys now worn by the USAF's fighter-optimised Eagle community. Wing and fuselage demarcation areas appear to be much the same, but the actual shadings used are markedly different. Weapons fit on both jets is identical, although the trailing aircraft has had its AIM-9M bolted onto the inner LAU-114 pylon*

Left *With fuel to burn, Gen McCloud stands 86-148 on its tail and gently climbs towards the stratosphere. In contrast to its heavily 'stickered' port intake, the jet carries a solitary 366th Wing badge to starboard. The Eagle's ability to 'make like a homesick angel' has long been one of its most impressive features, and in this light-weight fit, sustaining its legendary 50,000 ft per minute rate of climb shouldn't be too difficult up to more rarefied ceilings (Photo by Randy Jolly)*

Left *Inbound to intercept a strike package of marauding 389th FS F-16Cs heading for the Saylor Creek range, the 'Eagle Driver' keeps his visor down to reduce the levels of glare whilst scanning the horizon for the 'enemy'. He is wearing a standard issue lightweight HGU-55/P helmet that has been individually form-fitted to reduce the noise levels in the earphones, and a face-hugging oxygen mask*

Above *Well in the groove for a regulation touchdown and roll out down the Mountain Home runway, 86-161 was one of the last F-15Cs issued to the 390th FS, and as such was still to receive the unit's distinctive blue fin stripe when this shot was taken. The predominantly glassfibre honeycomb airbrake is raised for landing by a solitary hydraulic ram air jack that pushes through a titanium forging, the latter adding strength to the whole assembly. Although its sheer size makes it very effective for the role in which it was designed, it also successfully blocks the pilot's rearward vision once deployed*

CHAPTER TWO

391st FIGHTER SQUADRON

Below *The 391st FS, nicknamed the 'Bold Tigers', shares a similar history with the 390th FS, although its previous role within the 366th TFW was as the F-111A training squadron, as opposed to the latter's specialist 'Spark Vark' tasking. The squadron has 12 F-15Es on its books, all of which are labelled Primary Aircraft Authorised, which means that they would be in the vanguard of any 366th operational deployment at a time of crisis*

Left *Although similar in appearance to the F-15D, the E-model is more than just a dark grey Eagle that can drop bombs, as this head-on shot shows. It is a multi-role, all-weather, strike interdictor with a sophisticated bolt-on array of 'after market' sensor equipment that alloys it drop precision ordnance on the most difficult of targets. With its 'mud moving' role has come an increase in the jet's maximum take-off weight – 81,000 lbs compared with 68,000 lbs for an F-15C with CFTs fitted. As the latter are rarely used thanks to the Eagle's impressive range on internal fuel, a typical F-15C launches at a weight of 44,630 lbs – almost half the weight of a Strike Eagle*

Above Emphasising the truly rounded concept of the 'composite wing', members of the 366th pore over target photos and flight maps during the briefing for a forthcoming strike mission that will involve elements from all three outfits. In the foreground are 1st Lts Jeff Hubbell and Mark Dubois, Weapons Systems Officers (WSOs) from the 391st, who are conversing with an EF-111 Electronic Warfare Officer (EWO) from the newly-redesignated 429th Electronic Combat Squadron (ECS) and an F-16 'driver' from the 389th FS. The strength of the controversial 'Super Wing' can be seen in this photograph – crews from the 'component parts' of a strike package actually briefing together in one place at one time, rather than separately discussing their own particular roles in the impending sortie hundreds of miles apart at their different air bases

Right Just how newly-redesignated the 429th ECS was when this shot was taken in late 1992 is revealed by a close scrutiny of the sleeves of these nomex-suited individuals – both still wear old 390th ECS 'electronic boar' patches, denoting the unit's very recent connection with Mountain Home. Although based at Cannon AFB, New Mexico, with the F-111-equipped 27th FW (which has now all but transitioned to F-16C/Ds), the EF-111s are regular participants in 366th Wing exercises

This spread *Whilst the aircrew thrash out the minutiae of the impending sortie, the squadron groundcrews are bombing up the aircraft allocated for the flight. Using a vast array of purpose-built equipment like the MGI truck for the Universal Ammunition Loading System, technicians can bomb up an F-15E in what seems next to no time. These airmen are taking part in an Integrated Combat Turn (ICT), which sees their every move scrutinised by a team of Standardization Evaluators flown into Mountain Home without prior warning to check that aircraft turn-arounds are up to USAF standards.*

The 'loadies' have exactly 60 minutes to fully uplift all the ordnance and reload the aircraft's M61A1 20 mm Vulcan cannon. These weapons are inert 2000-lb Mk 84 LDGP (Low Drag General Purpose) 'iron' bombs, filled with concrete as denoted by the blue stripe around their noses – a yellow stripe signifies live ordnance. Once the driver has accurately positioned the bomb beneath the securing lugs he will get the signal to gently raise the lifting arm on the trolley so that the armourers can secure the ordnance to the pylon without actually having to take the strain of the weapon itself

Above *Gun-loading technicians wait for the bomb armourers to finish under the fuselage before moving into replenish the Vulcan cannon. Again, a special motorised trolley aids in completing this task as swiftly as possible – just as well really, as the centrally-placed magazine drum, which houses 940 rounds of 20 mm ammunition, is loaded as a complete unit, and is very heavy in weight. The jet's engines are often fired up and left idling during gun reloading as its internal hydraulic system can then be used to engage the new belts of ammunition into the Vulcan cannon itself*

Above right *The MGl truck can be adapted to handle virtually all external ordnance, as this wide-angle ramp shot clearly shows. Once the groundcrew have finished their 'conference', the missile-toting loader will be driven up beneath the port wing launch rail and the AIM-9M carefully raised until it is close enough to man-handle onto the aircraft*

Right *Occasionally 'brute force and ignorance' are brought into play when arming up a jet prior to launch, particularly if all the MGls are employed carrying heavier ordnance to waiting aircraft. This tow-trolley is equipped with special Sidewinder carriage cradles, which allow up to six fin-equipped rounds to be transported out to the ramp from the base armoury in one hit*

Above *Aside from its excellent reliability, relatively cheap price and 'fire-and-forget' delivery profile, one of the Sidewinder's major plus points is its light weight – the AIM-9M variant weighs in at 86 kgs. Granted, this particular round lacks both its motor and warhead (the heaviest parts of a Sidewinder), but the photograph nevertheless illustrates that a frontline fighter can be easily uploaded with the AIM-9 even if dedicated equipment like the MGI is unavailable. The F-15 is perhaps one of the most difficult of modern fighters to load a Sidewinder onto as the shoulder pylon is a good eight feet off the ground*

Opposite *Whilst the 'loadies' are getting on with their tasks at ramp level, the remaining members of the groundcrew will be dealing with myriad checks in the F-15E's state-of-the-art cockpits. Although the aircraft has its own Auxiliary Power Unit (APU) which can be used to charge up the electronics in the jet prior to engaging the F100s, engineers will always employ a ubiquitous A/MA 32A-60A 'huffer' if available, thus keeping the Strike Eagle's internal power supply fully charged up in*

case of emergency. Essentially a low-revving diesel generator dedicated to emitting sufficient power settings to fire up the jet's vast electronic suite, the 'huffer' also doubles as a 'starter motor' thanks to its ability to feed compressed air into the engines to get the latters' fan blades turning to a sufficient rpm, prior to the pilot commencing his ignition sequence from the cockpit.

In these views, the 'huffer' is obscured by another piece of ramp 'debris', the portable C-10 airconditioning unit, which is hooked up to the jet prior to the A/MA 32A-60A. This is a vital piece of kit as the ramp temperature at Mountain Home can easily top 35°C+ in the summer, which, in combination with the internal heat given off by the aircraft's systems, can quickly cause the F-15E's electronics to 'topple over'

Left For decades shod exclusively with Goodyear products from Akron, Ohio, many of the USAF's frontline types now boast tyres of French origin, as this tiger-striped main-gear hub clearly shows. Each tyre is inflated to 340 lbs/in^2, and is carefully monitored after each landing for tread wear and wall chafing

Below left *Although the 'groundies' are undoubtedly proficient at their respective jobs in preparing an aircraft for flight, it is still the aircrew who have to go 'burning and churning' in it at high-G out over the range. Therefore, all pilots and WSOs worth their salt will spend a good ten minutes on a preflight check, starting at the boarding ladder and working clockwise around the jet, shaking, pulling and pushing the machine's flying surfaces, wing pylons and ordnance. Pilots usually check the wings, tailplane, rudder and under-carriage, whilst the WSOs give the external stores the once-over.*

Here, Col Jerry Callen checks that the guidance fins on the AIM-9M dummy round fitted to 'his' jet have been secured correctly. Fitted to the same pylon is an SUU-20 dispenser, fully loaded with six BDU-33 'blue' bombs. This device, nicknamed the 'Sue' by air- and groundcrews alike, uses small explosive charges to eject the practice ordnance, and is also capable of carrying four 2.75 in rockets (note the quartet of firing ports). These are seldom carried in USAF service, however

Right *Satisfied that the stores won't prematurely depart company with the Strike Eagle, Callen takes one last look down the Volk Field flightline, prior to easing himself into his ACES II zero-zero ejector seat. Following him up the ladder is his WSO, Lt Bob Anderson*

Left It is essentially a two-man job to strap into a fast jet, as the pilot needs the aircraft's Dedicated Crew Chief (DCC) to pull his shoulder straps tight to restrict the former's body movement during high-G manoeuvring. The 'groundie' has to have the agility of a scaffolder to get in between the bulky ejection seat and the canopy in order to manipulate the Koch parachute straps to the pilot's satisfaction. Once this is done, he will go to work on the WSO, although he must perform the same task balanced on the intake lip due to the presence of the rear canopy framing behind the rear cockpit. Usually WSOs will strap in first in order to get the Honeywell ring-laser-gyro Inertial Navigation System (INS) prepped for immediate initialising once the engines are ignited — the INS can take up to ten minutes to complete this process in cold weather conditions (it usually takes just four, however), but once aligned this vital piece of mission equipment will provide accurate navigational readings as to the jet's precise location for the entire sortie

Above The DCC relies on a mike and headset patched into the jet's comms system to talk with the crew once the pilot has initiated engine spool up. The cord will be removed once the F100s are idling correctly, and the pilot and WSO are happy that all the jet's systems are functioning as advertised. Following a final visual check by the DCC to ensure that no fluid leaks have appeared since the engines ignited, he waves the F-15E out onto the taxyway

Above The tailplanes on these F-15Es seem to be waving at each other as the jets sit quietly on the Volk Field ramp opposite a quartet of 389th FS F-16Cs, all idling prior to roll out. Engine power provides hydraulic pressure for the fast jet's flight controls, duly 'flexing' the flying surfaces from their drooped static state. Once the engines shut down after a mission is completed, the compression in the hydraulics slowly leaks from the system and gravity takes hold – ailerons and tailplanes are particularly susceptible to 'ramp droop'

Left Like all 366th Wing assets, F-15E 87-202 is maintained in immaculate condition, the 391st 'Bold Tigers' stripes standing out well against its overall dark grey scheme. The Strike Eagle pioneered this one shade camouflage finish in the mid-1980s, and all 209 airframes delivered have stuck rigidly to it. Since then the B-1B, B-52 and F-111 have adopted a similar scheme, camouflage experts claiming that this particular shade of grey offers the best low observability rate during night/adverse weather missions from both the ground and the air.

All 12 F-15Es delivered to the squadron in the spring of 1992 came from the 4th Wing at Seymour Johnson, the latter being the first frontline outfit to be equipped with Strike Eagles. As such, the 391st operates some of the oldest F-15Es (Lot II aircraft) in service, although a handful of Lot IV machines are also on the squadron books. This particular Strike Eagle was the 34th airframe built at St Louis in the 42-strong Lot II batch, and previously served with the 335th FS

Above Col Jerry Callen leads his three-ship package along the Volk Field taxyway minutes away from launch. Beneath either intake is the podded Martin Marietta (Lockheed Martin) LANTIRN (Low Altitude Navigation and Targeting Infra-Red for Night) system, which bestows upon the F-15E an all-weather precision ordnance delivery capability unmatched by other strike aircraft in service in the 1990s. The larger pod (on the right) is the AAQ-14 targeting system, which contains a magnifying FLIR (Forward Looking Infr-Red) and laser in its nose. Both are housed in a fully mobile mounting which can remain boresighted on a target in virtually all hemispheres. The technology embodied within this pod is quite mind-boggling, the system benefiting from having its own range and control computers, plus full interface with the aircraft's APG-70 radar. Myriad technical and reliability problems initially beset the AAQ-14, resulting in its late delivery to the USAF.

The smaller AAQ-13 navigation pod proved to work as advertised virtually from the word go, and received clearance for service use three years earlier than the AAQ-14. It comprises a Texas Instruments terrain avoidance/following radar (TFR) in the bullet fairing, and a broad-view FLIR used purely to aid in night/bad weather flying. A similar LANTIRN system is also available for fitment to suitably-modified F-16Cs

Above *Half a dozen CBU-87s filled with live bomblets make up the offensive weaponry bolted onto 87-202 as it taxies out at the start of a CAS/BAI profile mission. The cluster bomb units each contain an SUU-65 dispenser filled with 202 BLU-97 combined effect munitions (CEMs). The latter are each the size and shape of a beer can, and are stabilised after ejection by a tail-mounted ballute. The weapon's warhead is shaped to aid penetration of a soft-skinned target, whilst its body explodes into anti-personnel and incendiary fragments*

Right *Toting both Mk 82 LDGPs and a quartet of AIM-9Ms, these two F-15Es personify the multi-role capability embodied in the Strike Eagle. This attribute has made the training of crews for the jet quite a complex affair as they have to be instructed in both ground attack and aerial combat prior to being posted to a frontline unit. Although primarily optimised to knock out ground targets, the F-15E will invariably be sent into hostile territory without a dedicated fighter escort as it is far more capable of defending itself against modern aerial threats than its predecessors, the F-111 or F-4. Therefore, it may be called upon to act as a fighter, shooting its way into and out of the target area. If this scenario arises, crews have to decide at which point to revert from fighter to attack mode in order to complete their primary task. This vexing question is often 'asked' by opposing USAF F-15s and F-16s during exercises at Red and Maple Flags, and so far the Strike Eagle's overwhelming ability, allied with crews of the highest calibre, has seen the jet rarely forced to compromise in either area over the range (Photo by Randy Jolly)*

Above *As if to prove that steering a fighter on the ground has nothing to do with inputs on the control column, the pilot of 87-202 is captured on film using both hands to adjust his helmet visor. Behind him, the WSO is head down 'house-keeping' on his four Multi-Function Displays (MFDs) prior to take-off, thus ensuring that he is ahead of the game with his systems primed and ready for launch. Notice how the intake has 'nodded' forward at a full take-off deflection angle of 11 degrees below the horizontal. The intakes are automatically programmed by the jet's data base to rotate to this deflection as soon as the F-15 spools up its engines on the flightline, thus allowing the airflow to pass uninterrupted into the twin F100s despite the Strike Eagle's increased angle of attack (AoA) at lift off*

Left *The F-15E grew out of a company-sponsored initiative to sell the USAF an F-111 replacement for the late 1980s, and official Air Force interest finally took the form of the Tactical All-Weather Requirement Study (TAWRS) which commenced in 1978. Its initial findings recommended that the USAF would be best served by purchasing more F-111Fs, the much-maligned General Dynamics design having fully matured into a potent precision weapon of war by this stage in its career. However, rumoured political wrangling eventually saw the Strike Eagle put forward as the best jet for the job, and the St Louis production line geared up to commence work on pre-production machines.*

Although outwardly similar to the F-15D, the F-15E's internals have been considerably 'beefed up' to withstand 9g manoeuvring with heavy loads. Indeed, up to 60 per cent of its structure was re-engineered, and its fatigue life duly raised to an incredible 16,000 hours. The jet further benefited from improved technology in the form of a Lear Astronics digital flight control system that was fitted in place of the fighter's analog equipment. Its triple-redundancy makes the Lear Astonics system ultra safe for low-level terrain-following sorties, being slaved to the TFR radar to allow the jet to be flown 'hands off' at tree-top height (Photo by Randy Jolly)

Above *Having topped his tanks up on the way to the range, the 391st's CO sits back and watches the progress of his wingman as the latter 'flies the boom'. Both jets are carrying inert laser-guided bombs, the closest aircraft toting four GBU-10 Paveway II 2000 'pounders', and the tanking machine six GBU-12A Paveway II 500 'pounders'. The blue-painted bombs denote that the casings are filled with concrete rather than explosives (Photo by Randy Jolly)*

Right Devoid of stores, a trio of Strike Eagles practise their refuelling skills with one of the 366th Wing's dedicated KC-135R tankers high over Idaho. The jet on the boom is a Gulf War veteran, having flown operationally from Al Kharj Air Base in Saudi Arabia with the 335th TFS, part of the 4th TFW (Provisional). Indeed, a number of the 391st's older F-15Es saw combat with the wing in Desert Storm

Below 87-208 is yet another jet to have dropped bombs in anger, and is seen here leading 88-667 aways from Saylor Creek following a bombing run with BDU-48s. The latter jet was the first of 42 Lot III F-15Es delivered to the USAF, who initially assigned it to the 336th TFS 'Rocketeers' at Seymour Johnson in 1989. Whilst in North Carolina the Strike Eagle wore the unit's famous yellow fin tip stripe, but this was soon replaced by the more garish 'tiger print' of the 391st FS once the F-15E was transferred to Mountain Home in 1992. This novel decoration was designed specially for the Strike Eagle, the 391st's F-111s having previously boasted just a simple blue fin stripe (Photo by S/Sgt Ron Mihu)

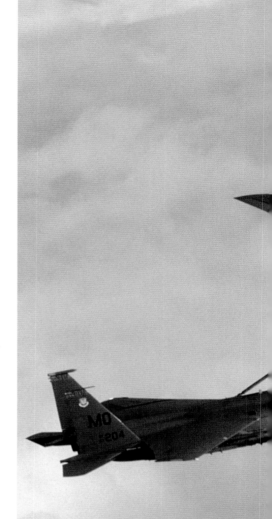

Inset No doubt feeling a little stiff after completing their strike sortie on Saylor Creek, the pilot and WSO extricate themselves from the jet and clamber back down its in-built boarding ladder to the ramp. The matt-finished paint quickly scuffs up around the ladder and cockpit sides on the F-15E primarily through it coming into contact with rubber-soled boots worn by air- and groundcrews

Left Mission accomplished, Capts Jones and Wright have taxied their jet back into the appropriate spot on the flightline, and now just await the word from the DCC over the intercom to shut the engines down. As with pre-flight checks, the post-flight procedure follows a defined checklist to ensure that all systems are correctly switched off, external stores rendered inert and ejection seats made safe. Only when all this has been completed will the crew be allowed to alight from their now silent steed and fill out the jet's Form 781, denoting any technical discrepencies that have flared up during the sortie. These 'write ups' will then provide an accurate guide for any rectification work that has to be carried out by squadron engineers prior to the jet being cleared for its next sortie

Laden down with their helmet bags, which also double as general 'hold-alls', Strike Eagle crews saunter back to the squadron offices where they will drop off their g-suit and bonedomes in the Life Support room prior to sitting down with a beer or a coffee for a mission debrief. Being a two-man jet, the F-15E fosters excellent camaraderie between pilot and WSO, who tend to team up early on in a tour and then stick together throughout their time with the unit

389th FTR SQ

CHAPTER THREE

389th FIGHTER SQUADRON

Left *The 'Universal Soldiers' of the 366th are the 24 F-16C/Ds of the 389th TFS, the Lockheed (formerly General Dynamics) fighter-bombers being capable of under-taking virtually any mission thrust upon the 'Gunfighters' as part of its global troubleshooting role. Pilots assigned to the Fighting Falcon community at Mountain Home undertake arguably the broadest remit of tasks allocated to any F-16-equipped unit in today's Air Force. For example, a typical Green or Red Flag exercise may see the jets configured purely as 'iron bombers', tasked with hitting a POL site or truck park. During this sortie, they will be adequately covered by 390th FS Eagles, so can focus purely on being 'mud movers'.*

On the next trip they may be assigned to protect intruding F-15Es or, very occa-sionally, B-1Bs from marauding 'enemy' forces — indeed, during the wing's first ever exercise in mid-1992, the 366th's B-52s were assigned to hit targets on the Fallon ranges, in Nevada, which were protected by US Navy F/A-18s. As the 390th FS had insufficient F-15Cs then on strength to cover the 'BUFFs', the 389th FS was given the task, on top of which they had to drop their own ordnance on designated targets during the very same sortie!

A recent airframe swap of its older Block 25 F-16Cs for the very latest Block 52D variants has seen the unit also acquire the ability to perform 'Wild Weasel' SAM sup-pression missions — another string to the jet's bow. Add to these roles the Fighting Falcon's legendary 'cheapness', both in terms of its purchase price and day-to-day operating costs, and it soon becomes obvious why the 389th FS is the most versatile component of the 366th Wing

Inset *As with the 390th and 391st FSs, the 389th has a long and distinguished history within the the 366th Wing stretching back to its inception in 1943 as a Fighter Group. Nicknamed the 'Thunderbolts', the unit's emblem has been gently cus-tomised since its re-equipment with the F-16 to give the 'bolt more of a falcon-like appearance!*

Right *Contrasting tail markings distinguish the Wing Commander's jet from a 'line' F-16C at Volk Field. The squared off fairings at either end of the rudder house antennae for the Itek AN/ALR-69 radar warning receiver (RWR). The horizontal ridges at the base of the fin are unique to the F-16C (and ADF versions of the A-model), and were a design mod forced upon General Dynamics in order to allow the relocated hydraulic accumulators to fit side by side within this narrow housing. On the F-16A/B the cylindrical accumulators sit on top of each other in the smaller fin root fillet, but this space has now been enlarged on the C/D and filled with power amplifiers for the RWR*

Opposite *Although the squadron's F-16s all wear the standard two-tone grey scheme adopted by the USAF right from the start of the jet's service life back in the late 1970s, the two 'boss birds' of the 389th have their fin codes applied in this rather unique fashion. Rather than have the lighter shade providing the drop-shadow, the jets use black as the infill (rather than white or light grey) for a mid-grey code applied in a similar shade to other 389th FS F-16s. Few, if any, F-16s have been spotted wearing similar non-regulation markings on their fins, and its attributes as a cotribution to low visibility are rather spoilt by the full-colour ACC badge and unit fin flash.*

83-132 was one of the very first F-16Cs built at Dallas/Fort Worth, being the eighth airframe in the Block 25A batch (serials 83-1135 to -1140) delivered to the USAF in early 1985. Unlike most other early-build F-16Cs in this production block which were issued to the then 363rd TFW (now 20th FW) at Shaw AFB, in South Carolina, this jet was sent to the elite 57th Fighter Weapons Wing (FWW) at Nellis. Here it performed trials work with new weapons recently cleared for frontline use, as well as undertaking experimental mission profiles out over the Red Flag ranges.

It was replaced by a brand new Block 52 machine in 1992 and sent to Mountain Home to join other Block 25A aircraft transferred in from Shaw. Here it remained until early 1994 when the 389th finally retired its venerable Block 25 jets – the last active-duty USAF unit to do so. These pristine machines in turn went to the 194th FS/144th FW of the California Air National Guard (ANG) at Fresno, where they replaced F-16A Block 15 ADFs. Back at Mountain Home, the 389th welcomed Block 52Ds, the most capable Fighting Falcons currently in USAF service

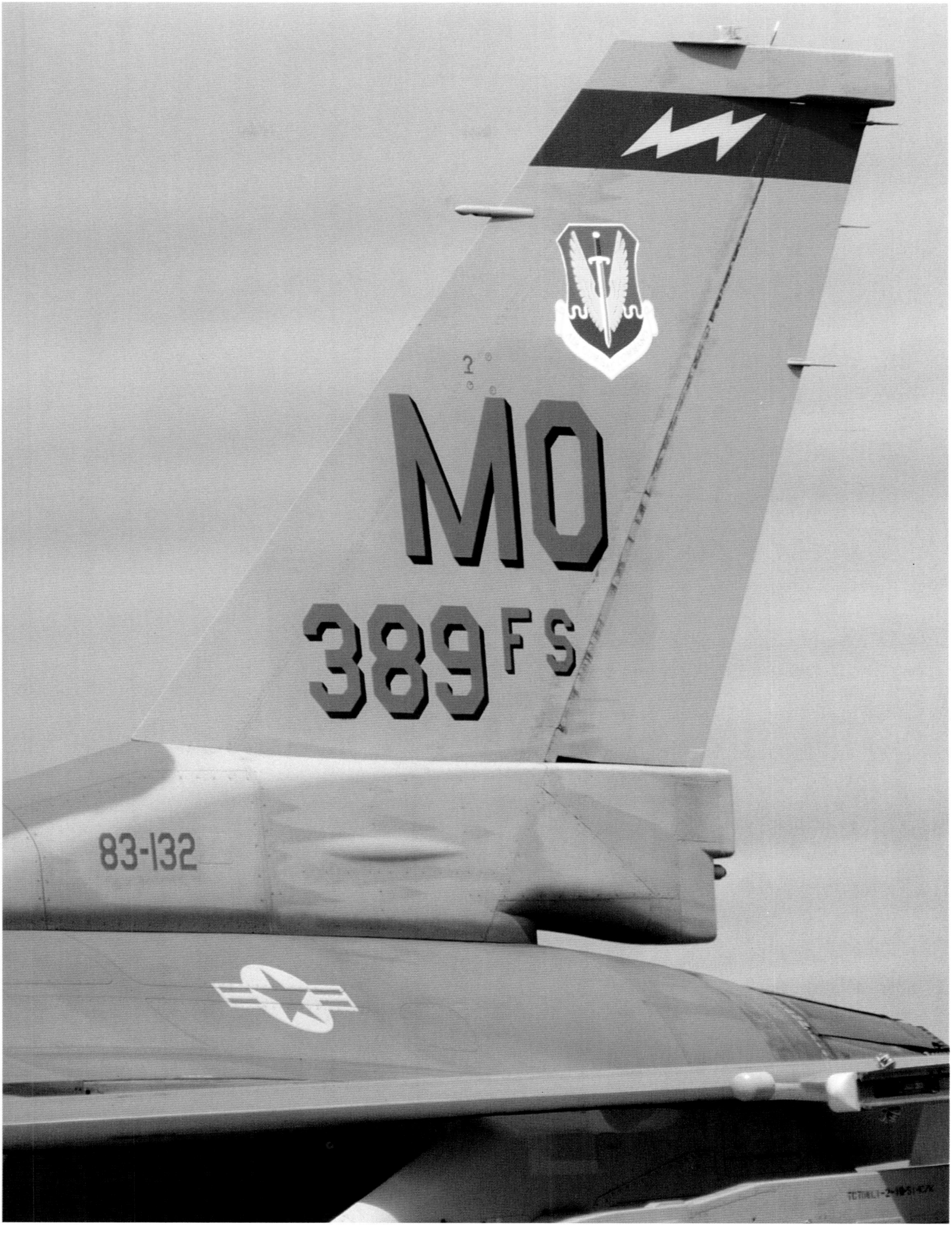
MO
389 FS
83-132

Above This jet has a variety of stores bolted onto it, including a concrete-filled (and very weathered) Mk 84 LDGP, Sidewinder acquisition round and a Westinghouse AN/ALQ-131(V) (deep) ECM pod. The latter device (and the newer AN/ALQ-184) is often seen on USAF F-16s as the fighter lacks its own integral ECM suite – it was decided early on in the jet's development that an internal system small enough to fit in the lithe F-16 would require the use of new technology that was not then available at a reasonable cost, and would delay the type's service entry should the USAF specify its fitment.

The ECM system is usually left to function automatically by the pilot once the fighter has entered enemy airspace, the fore and aft receivers monitoring all radar signals detected, and comparing their frequency parameters with a built-in threat library pre-progammed into the AN/ALQ-131. Once the signals have been analysed they are rapidly graded as to the threat they pose to the host aircraft, and the system in turn assigns jamming power from its various transmitters through power management techniques to 'blot out' the radar threat. Whilst continuing to search for other signals, the system monitors the effectiveness of the jamming it is presently

carrying out, and automatically changes power settings and frequencies should it deem that the primary threat is not being adequately neutralised

Above right DCC and pilot discuss the 'write ups' in the jet's Form 781 prior to the latter commencing his walkaround. Clearly visible beneath the fuselage is the ovoid 300 US gal centreline tank, designed specifically for this hardpoint on the F-16 to allow the external store to adequately clear the ground during taxying. When the jet is bombed and fuelled up the tank clears the ground by barely a foot

Right The ECM pod has taken the place of the centreline tank on this jet, as would invariably be the case should the 366th fly into combat. Outboard of the port 370 US gal wing tank is an inert AGM-65 Maverick air-to-surface missile, a favoured weapon for F-16s configured for precision anti-armour sorties. A handful of Maverick variants are available to USAF mission planners, fitted with a variety of seeker units and warheads

In order to keep the overall weight of the F-16 down to a bare minumum, General Dynamics built the jet without an integral boarding ladder. The USAF was therefore tasked with designing a special one-off design built specially for the F-16. As this sequence clearly shows, the device had to be contoured to avoid its fitment damaging the delicately sculptured forebody strakes, which sit out proud of the fuselage. Once the pilot has climbed the ladder he has to rather inelegantly straddle the cockpit sides and gently lower himself into the angled ACES II seat using his arms as levers. With the pilot safely ensconced in his 'office', the DCC climbs up to help him on with his parachute straps.

The narrow track of the lightweight undercarriage is clearly visible in this photographic sequence, its general layout and engineering having remained constant throughout the F-16's long production life. The bulged 'eyes' either side of the radom house the forward-hemisphere RWRs of the AN/ALR-69 system

Above With atmospheric conditions perfect for a Maverick strike on the Saylor Creek range, Capt Nate Thomas is helped into 84-378. Like the Sidewinder, an inert AGM-65 provides adequate realism for training purposes over the range once its optical or infra-red seeker head is uncaged and left to search out a target. The pilot monitors the missile's view of the target area through a centrally-mounted CRT between his legs, manipulating the Maverick's slaved sensor head through inputs on his HOTAS until the aiming mark on the screen straddles the target. He then selects lock-on and theoretically launches the round off the hardpoint – in practice the engineless store stays firmly attached to the wing pylon, thus allowing this routine to be followed over and over again.

The flat plain on which Mountain Home is built becomes starkly apparent in sunny weather, the peak ridge of the Idaho Mountain range running away in the distance. This Block 25E jet was issued to the 363rd TFW's 17th TFS, nicknamed the 'Hooters', in early 1985, and later flew 35 combat missions with this unit from Al Dafra Air Base in the United Arab Emirates during Desert Storm

Left Lt Col Tim Nall folds up his mission map prior to securing it in the cockpit of his jet and climbing aboard. His velcro and zipper-strewn 'speed jeans' firmly secured on his lower body, Nall relies on his decidedly 'low tech' flying boots to give him good purchase on the battered boarding ladder whilst perched astride the F-16. Immediately aft of the ladder is the jet's sole M61A1 20 mm Vulcan cannon

Above and right *All 389th FS 'jocks' wear a red skull cap underneath their 'bone domes', whilst F-15E crews don tiger-striped orange headwear! With his helmet securely done up, the pilot has begun to keyboard in his flight details – waypoints, headings, fuel weight, radio channel frequencies and IFF modes – on the 84-241's up-front control panel sited just beneath the GEC Avionics HUD. This panel is easily manipulated once in flight, flashing all the relevant mission data on the wide-angle HUD. Both this jet and the F-16C (84-223) parked alongside it saw action in the Gulf War with the 363rd TFW (Provisional), the former flying 46 missions adorned with the nickname* Hooter Standards, *and the latter 44 missions as* Hussein's Worst Nightmare *– both were 17th TFS machines*

Inset The yellow nose stripe on this Mk 84 LDGP 2000-lb bomb denotes that it is a live munition, and is to be treated with due care. It has been mated with a standard instantaneous/short delay M904 nose-mounted fuse, and the DCC is giving the weapon's securing lugs one final look over before removing the flagged T-key safety pin. With the latter pulled out the pylon is thus rendered live, and will eject the bomb when the pilot presses the weapons' release button on his HOTAS. Behind the DCC, the second 'groundie' is checking the covering of the port RWR blister

Left Satisfied that the Fighting Falcon is fully primed for the live bombing sortie that lays ahead, the groundcrew have pulled away the wheel chocks and left the jet to idle momemtarily before waving the pilot out on to the taxyway. The bulk of the centreline ECM pod is well illustrated here, the store weighing in at 573 lbs. Despite its girth, and cumbersome appearance, the AN/ALQ-131 was designed from the outset to be high-g rated – a great improvement over its predecessor, the AN/ALQ-119 store, which was speed-limited due to mach-induced flutter

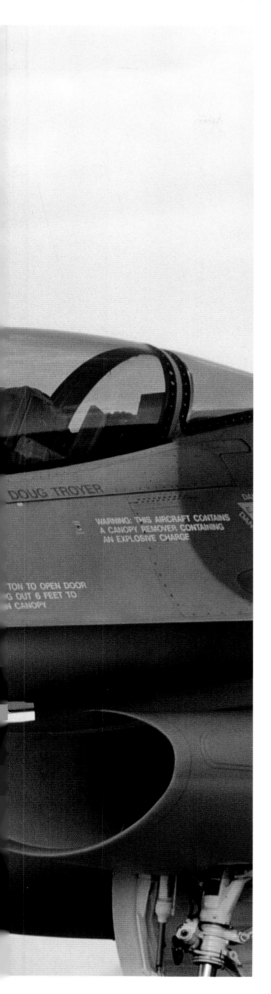

Above *Chocks safely in-hand, the 'Ray-Banned' airman keeps a watchful eye on his boss as the latter guides the pilot out onto the taxyway. Behind the jet 84-261 rumbles off towards the Arming Area, where its bombs will be rendered live. No stranger to live ordnance, -261 flew 40 missions with the 17th TFS as Blood Storm during the Gulf War*

Left *With the F100 idling smoothly and his HUD programmed with all the relevant information for the sortie, the pilot pauses momentarily to take in his surrounding whilst his squadron-mates complete their pre-taxying routines. The superb visibility offered by the two-piece canopy is self-evident from this angle, the forward and centre sections of the transparency being engineered from a single piece of polycarbonate. A constant 0.5 in thick, the canopy is built to withstand a four-pound birdstrike at 350 kts. Should the pilot lose his canopy entirely, the glass of the HUD unit is designed to shield him from the resulting slipstream, thus providing the pilot with an impromptu windscreen*

Inset *The heavy punch for this attack package will be provided by a quartet of F-15Es, which can also quickly switch roles should the F-16 escort find itself overwhelmed by Eagles as they near the target. This role duality by two of the three fighter squadrons within the 366th is encouraged by the wing's staff officers, and is often put into practice on the more high-profile stage of a Red or Green Flag exercise*

Left *Proving the versatility of the design, a quartet of 'slick' fighter-optimised 389th jets are launched simultaneously with the bomb-toting F-16s to ride 'shotgun' against the intercepting F-15Cs of the 390th FS. For this sortie the Eagle 'drivers' will have their interception ability downgraded to non-BVR in order to focus on short range ACM – a profile that allows the Fighting Falcons to take on their fighter-optimised brethren on a near-equal footing*

Right *Viewed from the back seat of a F-16D, a trio of F-16Cs await the signal to taxy out to the last chance checkpoint prior to launch. The closest jet has a fully-loaded SUU-20 pod on its outer hardpoint, plus an AIM-9M acquisition round on the wingtip rail and an AN/ALQ-131(V) ECM pod on the centreline station. These three jets flew a combined total of 133 missions in Desert Storm, with 84-243 topping the list with 51*

Devoid of any Remove Before Flight tags, and with their 'iron' bombs duly rendered live, five Fighting Falcons sit at the EOR awaiting launch clearance. Once the tower has signalled its approval, each pilot will advance his throttle to 85 per cent power, give the engine temperature on the CRTs one last check and engage nosewheel steering. The brakes are then released, power further increased by moving the throttle to mil (military power) and then, after a brief pause, afterburner is selected.

The pilot ensures that the HOTAS has full-forward pressure applied at 'brakes off', thus minimising drag and allowing him

to retain nosewheel steering in the event of tyre failure. As the jet passes through 100 kts (ten seconds after brake release) nosewheel steering is disengaged and full-back pressure is applied to the HOTAS. A further five or six seconds then pass by until the nose starts to point skyward, and with the F-16 bombed up in this configuration, it will begin to rotate at 160 kts. The pilot eases the HOTAS forward to maintain the jet's launch angle at five to ten degrees nose-high, and roughly five seconds later the F-16 is airborne at 180 kts. In peacetime, aircraft will usually launch ten to twenty seconds apart

Above *Afterburner aglow, 84-256 gathers speed on its climb out from Mountain Home. The undercarriage is seconds away from full retraction, with the intake-mounted nosewheel door being clearly visible as it motors up to its closed position. 'Gear up' is selected at 50 ft and 200+ kts, the former having to be stored away prior to their 250-kt speed limit mark being reached. The red cockpit light which is illuminated whilst the undercarriage is extended will usually extinguish at about 240 kts. Once gear-stowage has been safely dealt with, the pilot turns his attention to engine power settings, with the afterburner being deselected once the jet has attained a speed of 300 to 350 kts*

Opposite *Having put a few more craters in the already pock-marked landscape of Saylor Creek, the 389th FS pilots take it in turns to top up their tanks courtesy of a 22nd ARS KC-135R despatched specially for this mission. The ability to generate dedicated tanker support from within the 366th is a major plus point of the composite wing structure, making any potential strike package self-sufficient when it comes to planning a sortie. Other conventional wings have to go 'off-base' to request access to a tanker from an Air Mobility Command unit*

Following the completion of their tanking cycle, the pilots form up in an impeccable line abreast formation off the port wing of the tanker in order for the author to record the event for posterity from his back-seat vantage point in the F-16D. 84-213 has an inert Maverick round under its wing, whilst all four jets boast AN/ALQ-131(V) ECM pods

Right A 'boomer's eye' view of an F-16 closing on the tanker for gas. This jet is configured for ACM work only, lacking external tanks, and is therefore more likely to require the services of a KC-135 once its internal fuel supply runs low. Despite the design of the F-16 now being over two decades old, the jet hardly shows any real signs of ageing, particularly when viewed 'clean', head on. The unobstructed view offered to the pilot can be well appreciated from this angle

Below Strike leader Capt Rob 'Dools' Dooley has his turn on the boom in 84-217 whilst the rest of 'T-Bolt' Flight trail in the tanker's wake. The familiar two-tone grey shading featured on all frontline USAF F-16s is beautifully illustrated by the closest jet, 84-213. An ex-17th TFS machine, this war veteran completed 47 missions as Tazmanian Devil from Al Dafra during its Desert Storm tour in early 1991. Obviously well used by the 389th FS, the jet's distinctive red fin stripe is in dire need of a touch up

Above The pilot gently drops back behind the KC-135 once the refuelling has been completed – note that the receptacle door has yet to be closed on the spine. Although devoid of wing stores, bar the Sidewinder rounds, 84-252 is still equipped with a ubiquitous ECM pod, which rather mars its otherwise sleek profile. Along with 84-251, this jet flew the highest total of sorties by a 363rd TFW F-16 during Desert Storm, successfully completing 58 missions

Right Although some pilots initially find aerial refuelling a stamina-sapping task, like most things that require both physical and mental dexterity, practice makes perfect. The F-16 is one of the easiest jets in which to tank, with the centrally-mounted receptacle being fitted vertically in line with the cockpit. The pilot's angled ACES II ejector seat also allows him to keep a watchful eye on proceedings without unduly straining his neck muscles in the process. Finally, the frameless canopy obviates the need for the pilot to perform 'cockpit gymnastics' in order to see the traffic light arrangement built into the tanker's belly

This jet was photographed during a transit flight from Mountain Home to Volk Field, the small store between the port tank and outer wing pylon being an MXU-648 baggage pod which will contain crew essentials (spare clothes, tennis racket and golf clubs) for the det away from base. Despite the fancy designation, the MXU-648 is little more than a gutted BLU-1/27 firebomb shell, fitted with either a removeable tailcone or side door for internal access. Some units proudly decorate their -648s in full unit regalia, but this pod has had to make do with a uniform coat of gloss grey paint instead.

The Volk Field Combat Readiness Training Center is a 'bare bones' base, consisting of little more than taxyways, and a cluster of hangars. The 366th regularly use the facility to practise wing-strength deployments 'into the field', where they operate independently of their well-oiled base infrastructure back at Mountain Home – just as they would have to should an incident occur in the Middle East, the Balkans or Africa, where facilities available on the ground rarely match those on offer at a typical frontline USAF base

Right As noted earlier in this volume, the 389th FS recently replaced its veteran Block 25A F-16Cs with factory-fresh Block 52D machines, which are currently the most advanced frontline Fighting Falcons in USAF service. Externally little different from the unit's previous mounts, the new aircraft have the capability to perform the treacherous 'Wild Weasel' mission thanks to an updated systems fit which enables the jet to carry the Texas Instruments AN/ASQ-213 HARM (High-velocity Anti-Radiation Missile) podded Targeting System, in conjunction with the AGM-88 missile. Jets fitted with the bolt-on equipment allow the 366th to undertake dedicated SAM suppression without having to rely on 'Wild Weasel' units from other ACC wings.

This shots shows two of the wing's new jets on a Maverick training mission over a snowy Idaho in March 1994, the aircraft in the foreground having the added distinction of being not only the CO's personal mount, but also the very first Block 52D jet built at Fort Worth (Photo by Randy Jolly)

Left Although the AGM-88 is the favoured 'smart' weapon for handling SAM/radar sites, the much cheaper Maverick is just as effective at knocking out electronic targets should the opportunity arise. A Block 52 F-16C is virtually identical in terms of its offensive capability to the more common Block 50 machine, but they have different powerplants. The latter relies on the 29,000-lb thrust-rated General Electric F110-GE-129 IPE engine, but the former has a Pratt & Whitney F100-PW-229 IPE installed, giving the 389th FS spares compatibility with the 390th and 391st FSs, whose F-15s use the same powerplants (Photo by Randy Jolly)

Above All Fighting Falcon units have at least one F-16D 'twin tub' on strength to provide check rides and familiarisation on type for new pilots and VIPs alike. For a number of years 84-322 was one of a pair of D-models at Mountain Home, the jet being tasked with its fair share of bombing and ACM sorties just like the more abundant F-16Cs. This is consistent with the USAF requirement that all training variants of frontline fighters be fully mission-capable, the two-seater's only concession to its 'duality' being a reduction in its internal fuel capacity by 1500 lbs. Like most other 389th FS Block 25 jets, this aircraft originally served with the 363rd TFW

Right All manner of training and refresher sorties can be completed in the F-16D, the rear seat occupant in this machine re-acquainting himself with tanking after a spell 'out of the saddle'. His instructor up front has his hands visibly free of the HOTAS, thus ensuring that the 'boomer' is fully aware that the 'guy in back' is handling the hook up on this occasion

CHAPTER FOUR

HEAVY METAL

Left *For almost two years the 'big stick' within the 366th Wing was provided by seven B-52Gs of the 34th Bombardment Squadron (BS). Although assigned to Mountain Home, these jets remained at Castle AFB, in California, where they had previously served with the 93rd Bombardment Wing (BW). The primary reason for this was to avoid additional costs in enlarging the support and hangarage facilities required for the 'BUFF'. Nevertheless, equipment and men had to be regularly flown into the Idaho base to support B-52s on deployment to the 366th – a not inconsiderable task for ASC assets.*

The composite wing at Mountain Home was the first unit within the USAF to combine former TAC and SAC assets within the same structure, and the overwhelming firepower brought to the party by the former strategic bombers was soon appreciated by the more numerous fighter 'jocks'. 'They add a lot, providing a tremendous capability day or night. If we have to put iron on the target from Stateside, the "BUFFs" will be the first to go', commented then 391st FS CO Lt Col Robin Scott. This particular B-52G-120-BW, 59-2569, was finally retired to Davis-Monthan on 15 February 1994 following the 34th BS's re-equipment with B-1Bs. Thirty years earlier it had started its long USAF career with the 416th BW/668th BS at Griffiss AFB in New York, and had ended its spell in SAC in 1992 with the 328th Bombardment Training Squadron

Inset Aside from being some of the first ex-SAC assets to don ACC colours, the 'magnificent seven' 366th B-52s were also the premier users of the Martin Marietta AGM-142 Popeye conventional stand-off missile. A 'buy in' from Rafael Armament Development Authority of Israel through the 'Have Nap' programme, the 3300-lb weapon has a warhead of 1975 lbs and a range of 58 miles. A fire and forget round, the Popeye has its own inertial navigation system plus an electro-optical homing device for terminal guidance when in visual range of the designated target. Although a large missile, this live AGM-142 is rather dwarfed by its temporary host – just look at the size of the weapons rack!

Left Used to the mild California climate at Castle, a det to Mountain Home in the winter was an unpleasant experience particularly for groundcrews, as the worst of the Idaho weather could create conditions like this for an entire deployment. The crew of this 'BUFF' sit idling on the ramp whilst the myriad pre-taxy checks on all eight engines are completed. The two bulges on the chin of the jet house the AN/ASQ-151 Electro-Optical Viewing System (EVS), which helps the crew perform low-level sorties in poor light conditions, whilst the cheek blisters cover AN/ALQ-117 Radar Warning Receivers and the excrescence on the nose is the forward-hemisphere ALT-28 ECM antenna

Above With its starboard wing sitting over on its out-rigger, B-52G-90-BW 57-6520 shows signs of a recent repaint on its huge slab fin. The once-familiar SAC shield has benn replaced by an ACC decal, and the distinctive stylised 'castle' motif has been replaced with a 34th BS thunderbird on the fin tip. Note the fuselage rippling just forward of the wing leading-edge on this veteran jet, which was a common feature on all B-52s during their twilight years in USAF service (Photo by Brian C Rogers)

Right A closer view of the tail markings on 57-6520 reveals the subtle areas of overspray which signalled the end of an era for the once-proud SAC. This airframe was the last in the fourth batch (of 12) of G-models built for the USAF at Boeing's then new Wichita plant, and it entered service with the 39th BW/62nd BS at Eglin AFB, Florida, in the early 1960s. It was finally retired to Davis-Monthan on 27 January 1994. The fin bulge hides the rear-facing ALT-28 ECM antenna, whilst the notch in the leading edge is the ram air intake for the jet's APU (Photo by Brian C Rogers)

The launch of a B-52G was truly a stealthy event as it belched out so much smoke from its water-injected Pratt & Whitney J57-P-43WB turbojet engines that it was virtually masked from prying eyes on the ground. Looking like an ecological disaster, this jet rotates away from the Mountain Home runway, the pilot having just begun to cycle in the outriggers on the wing tips. The huge area of trailing-edge Fowler flap on the B-52 is clearly evident in this shot. 'BUFF' maintainers have fought a constant battle with cracked flaps during the jet's long service to its country, the combination of sonic noise energy and wing wake buffet producing destructive torsional stresses on the moveable wing area (Photo by George Hall/Check Six)

Above No photograph in this volume better illustrates the total force concept of the 366th Wing in its original form than this view of a 'MO' coded KC-135R and a varied array of 'clients' trailing the boom. Since this shot was taken in 1993, the B-52s have been replaced with B-1Bs and the EF-111As (based at Cannon AFB, but often seen at Mountain Home) threatened with retirement by 1998 – jointly-manned EA-6B Prowlers are scheduled to then inherit the overwhelming task of fulfilling USAF/US Navy ECM requirements (Photo by S/Sgt Mihu)

Right The positioning markings applied to the underside of the KC-135R are clearly visible in this shot of a 34th BS 'Bone' refuelling from a 22nd ARS tanker. Due to the B-1B's overwhelming unit cost, it is unlikely to be used simply as a 'blanket bomber' by the 366th in unsanitised airspace, and in its designed role as a low-level/high speed penetrator, it has to operate by itself in order to achieve the element of surprise. So where does that leave the seven B-1Bs of the 34th BS? The immediate answer to that question is tasked with restricted mission profiles that see the bomber operating as part of a larger strike package in peacetime exercises. However, with the USAF currently trying to accelerate its weapons clearance programme for the 'Bone', it should mean that B-1B crews will be able to deploy stand-off weapons similar to those previously available with the veteran 'BUFF' (Photo by Randy Jolly)

Left A thirsty B-52 can stay hooked up behind a KC-135 for well over 30 minutes, seriously denting the tanker's load of JP-4. Being positioned so close to the nose of the jet, a 'BUFF' pilot finds it quite easy to complete the approach and hook up with the Stratotanker, although the 'bow wave' created by his large mount can cause the boom to move around rather more than if he was flying a smaller fighter. The size and shape of the RWR and ECM blisters scabbed onto the B-52G are clearly shown in this view

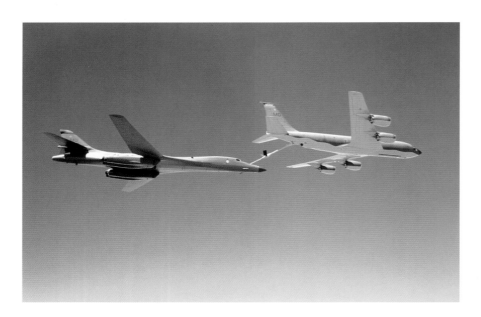

Right *Now but a distant memory in the pattern over Mountain Home, the B-52Gs were well-respected by the senior officers of the 366th, and in some ways were more mission-capable in terms of the wing's composite structure than the 34th BS's present mount, the B-1B. The amalgamation of former SAC and TAC ways has taken time to mesh at the 366th, and more problems than successes have perhaps been thrown up in the first four years of the wing's existence. However, the working relationship achieved between fighter pilots and 'BUFF' crews was a positive one: with the challenge of integrating the latter's capabilities (stand-off missile attacks and volumic 'iron' bomb delivery) into what was essentially a TAC wing structure having been finally sorted out just in time for the B-52Gs to be retired in favour of the B-1B, with its vastly different mission profile!*

Above *With the change in equipment came a change in base for the 34th BS, the unit moving to Ellsworth, South Dakota, where it inherited jets from the incumbent 28th BW. Being 'stuffed full' of complex weapons, ECM and navigation systems, it made sense to keep the 'Bone' sited in a location where all the expertise and service back up was readily on call. However, 'MO'-coded B-1Bs can regularly be spotted on the ramp at Mountain Home, and the unit operates totally independently of the remaining two 'Bone' units at Ellsworth (Photo by Randy Jolly)*

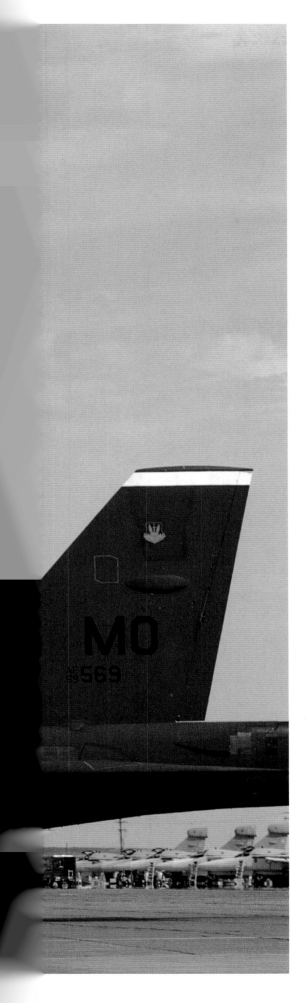

THEY ALSO SERVE

Left *Two of the three types visible in this shot no longer grace the ramp at Mountain Home. The B-52 wears a white stripe on its tail, a marking not associated with any SAC/ACC unit known to this author. Perhaps it was photographed in an interim stage prior to the 34th BS's thunderbird being applied in red over the top. This theory is lent more credence by the solid bottle green fin stripe on the KC-135R parked in the foreground. Subsequent photos of this machine showed that the word 'Gunfighters' was stencilled in yellow over the green base colour in an appropriate 'Wild West' typeface*

Above *KC-135R 63-8004 displays its definitive tail art in this close up view. The first KC-135As delivered to the USAF back in the late 1950s were fitted with a shorter fin and manually-operated rudder, which made them hard work to fly over long periods, but Boeing soon increased the fin area with the fitment of a powered rudder. In the 1980s the USAF embarked on a mammoth re-finning programme which saw virtually the entire 700-strong KC-135 fleet fitted with ex-commercial 707/720 vertical surfaces in order to prolong the life of the heavily-tasked tanker force well into the 21st century (Photo by Randy Jolly)*

Left *The angle of this impressive air-to-air view seems to make the already 'fat' General Electric/SNECMA F108-CF-100 turbofan engines that distinguish the KC-135R from the rest of the Stratotanker pack even more portly! Although an 'R' may lack the spectacle of a water-injection smoke screen to accompany its take-off roll, once in the air the jet is far more 'fighter-like' to fly thanks to the immense reserves of power on call should the pilot choose to throttle up the quartet of turbofans, each of which is rated at 24,000 lbs thrust – the P & W J57-P-39W could crank out 13,750 lbs with water injection on a mild day! 61-277 came to Mountain Home from 340th ARW at Altus AFB, Oklahoma (Photo by Randy Jolly)*

Inset *Only 62-3513 shows no signs of a hasty touch-up job following its transfer to the 22nd ARS in this ramp shot. Unlike the fighter and bomber types in the 366th, which tended to come from one single unit, the six KC-135Rs assigned to the wing were picked from a number of sources; 62-3513 formerly served with the 305th ARW at Grissom AFB, Indiana, 62-3572 (the last of the trio converted from A to R specs in 1992) hailed from the 384th ARS at McConnell AFB, Kansas, and 63-8004 from the 92nd ARS at Fairchild AFB, Washington*

Inset *As mentioned earlier, mission planners at the 366th realise just how fortunate they are to have six tankers dedicated to their needs on a 24-hour basis, and most strike packages put up by the wing include a refuelling cycle in order to make full use of this asset. This 'Tiger Flight' quartet from the 391st FS caught up with the 22nd ARS's 'boss bird' soon after peppering Saylor Creek with CBUs*

Right *This is a familiar view for the fighter and bomber pilots of the 366th, particularly when the wing is deploying to a Green or Red Flag exercise, or perhaps travelling even further to Volk Field. Although the four most obvious differences between a KC-135A and an R are hanging under the wings, internally things are rather more modern also. The latter jet has a dual auxiliary power unit (APU) quick-start system, Turbine Engine Monitoring System (TEMS), Flight Control Augmentation System (FCAS), Air Data Computer (ADC) and Mk III anti-skid five-rotor disc brakes coupled with a more robust landing gear. All of these improvements have revolutionised the humble old 'Strat', meaning that it will continue to shoulder the burden of USAF tanking tasks on a global basis for many years to come*

Inset *As with the maintenance-intensive B-1B, the 366th nominally has three E-3B/C Sentry AWACS on strength, although these are based at Tinker AFB, Oklahoma, so that they can have their myriad systems looked after by the dedicated maintenance crews of the 552nd Airborne Control Wing (ACW). The wing has suffered due to a lack of E-3 support on exercises and deployments – the demand placed on the AWACS by the USAF both in CONUS and abroad has stretched the 552nd to near breaking point as the 1990s have progressed. Four frontline units and a solitary training squadron share 32 E-3s between them, each outfit marking its jets with a fin stripe – red denotes an E-3 from the 964th ACS*

Main picture *Few would argue with the combat ability of the aircraft featured in this shot, either in the 'mud moving' or air superiority roles. The versatility of the 366th sets new challenges for a Mission Commander, as the designated strike leader has to think more broadly along the lines of what the different types of aircraft in his package can achieve singularly, and how they can be best employed to ensure overall mission success. Capt Rob 'Dools' Dooley, formerly of the 389th FS, explains how he tackled the job whilst he was based at Mountain Home in the following passage;*

'As Mission Commander, you're not out to create the world by yourself. You're there to bring the people together and manage

them to create it for you. That's pretty critical when you have a mission that involves so many different types of aircraft. I'm far from being an expert on how an F-15E will want to attack its assigned target, but the F-15E representative that plans the mission with me is going to tell me their best tactic. The same goes for the B-52s (now B-1Bs). The F-15Cs flight leader is going to be Air-to-Air commander for the mission, and will develop the best tactic that will attrit the enemy fighter, and thus protect the package. You've got to rely on the expertise from the component parts of the package, take all their inputs and meld it all together to achieve the objectives for the mission. However, overall you're the ultimate decision maker.

'When you're airborne you've got to worry about your own flight, and trust that everyone else is flying the plan according to what was briefed. I also have the power to terminate the sortie, or put the attack on hold should an emergency arise in-flight like airspace restrictions or a shifting battle line since we launched.

'The slick thing about the Composite Wing at Mountain Home is that we all pretty much know all the other guys in the different squadrons on a first name basis. And this familiarity soon gets you "smart" on what their jets can and cannot do, so when it comes time to fly a mass package, the planning phase of the mission tends to move along a lot smoother than what may occur elsewhere' (Photo by Randy Jolly)

Left and above The 'bean counters' on Capitol Hill have slowly stripped USAF assets back to the bone through swingeing budget cuts since the end of the Gulf War, and one of their primary targets has been single-mission types. Ironically enough, in a time of war one of the first elements to appear on a Mission Commander's 'must have' list of supporting types is the EF-111A Raven, which has the proven ability to render an enemy blind electronically.

As mentioned previously, Mountain Home has a strong tie to the venerable 'Spark Vark' as it was home to the 24-strong 390th ECS from 1981 through to 1993, which was tasked with providing ECM support for much of the USAF. With the creation of the 366th Wing, the EF-111As flew south to Cannon AFB, New Mexico, the last home of the American 'Earth Pig'. However, despite the type's impeccable war record and undisputed ability to still 'fry' the best radar systems ranged against it by any potential aggressor, the EF-111 has lost the 'war' on the domestic front due to its astronomical operating costs – the basic airframes are now almost 30 years old, and with the 'straight' F-111 bomber now phased out of service, the associated spares stock hold is no longer as plentiful as it once was. The end result is that the surviving EF-111As are due for retirement to Davis-Monthan by no later than 1998

Left and above *The previous caption is equally as applicable to these shots of a specialist type highly valued by the men at the 'pointy end' once the @*ª¢ starts flying, but discarded by individuals who wage war with a cost spread sheet. The F-4G 'Wild Weasel' is of a comparable vintage to the Raven, and like the latter, was a regular participant flown into Mountain Home for 366th strike exercises by the Boise-based 190th FS of the Idaho ANG. This arrangement suited both parties fine, as it meant that the 'weekend warriors' got to operate in a frontline environment with the active duty squadrons, and the 366th could add another string to its independent strike package bow. Again, the F-4G has now been consigned to history, the 'Wild Weasel' role having been partly filled by the 389th FS's AGM-88-capable Block 52 F-16Cs*

When planning the composite wing, USAF staff officers not only had to bear in mind the offensive capabilities of the 366th, but also the support needed to keep the outfit airworthy should they have to deploy at short notice across the globe. A major headache was solved on the engineering front when it was decided that all three fighter squadrons would fly aircraft powered by the same type of engine – the ubiquitous Pratt & Whitney F100-PW-220. Aircraft downtime through mechanical problems has never been a major problem in the 366th thanks to this, the spares supply system working with model efficiency on base. Equally, when the wing deploys on exercise, it is a simple task to load several C-5s up with engine test equipment and parts held in stock that are applicable to all three FSs

APPENDICES

SERIALS OF CURRENT TYPES EQUIPPING THE 366th WING

389th FIGHTER SQUADRON

F-16C Fighting Falcon
91-0362, 91-0370, 91-0386, 91-0392, 91-0393, 91-0401,
91-0413, 92-3880, 92-3881, 92-3882, 92-3885, 92-3888,
92-3889, 92-3890, 92-3896, 92-3898, 92-3899, 92-3908,
93-0541, 93-0545

F-16D Fighting Falcon
91-0466, 91-0473, 91-0475, 91-0479

390th FIGHTER SQUADRON

F-15C Eagle
85-0127, 85-0128, 86-0143, 86-0144, 86-0145, 86-0146,
86-0148, 86-0149, 86-0150
('366th WG'-marked a/c),
86-0151, 86-0152, 86-0155, 86-0157 ('390th FS'-marked a/c),
86-0158, 86-0161, 86-0162, 86-0168, 86-0170, 86-0179

F-15D Eagle
86-0181

391st FIGHTER SQUADRON

F-15E Strike Eagle
87-0169, 87-0170, 87-0173, 87-0182 ('366th WG'-marked a/c)
87-0183, 87-0198, 87-0201, 87-0202, 87-0204, 87-0207, 87-0208, 87-0209,
87-0210 ('391st FS'-marked a/c), 88-1667, 88-1697, 88-1705, 88-1707,
89-0487, 89-0497, 89-0506

34th BOMB SQUADRON

B-1B Lancer
85-0091, 86-0097, 86-0104, 86-0116, 86-0118, 86-0121, 86-0125, 86-0131,
86-0134 ('34th BS'-marked a/c), 86-0138, 86-0139

22nd AIR REFUELING SQUADRON

KC-135R
59-1475 ('22nd ARD'-marked a/c), 19-1498, 60-0365, 61-0277, 62-3513, 62-3572, 63-8004

T-37B
59-0294, 60-0177, 64-3418

Left *The inner sanctum of the flightline is protected by the ubiquitous orange rope familiar to USAF military aircraft enthusiasts the world over . . . and a couple of dozen fully-armed military police cruising the base in HUMVEEs*

SPECIFICATIONS FOR CURRENT AIRCRAFT TYPES

ROCKWELL B-1B LANCER

Wing: span 136 ft 8.5 in (41.67 m) spread and 78 ft 2.5 in (23.84 m) swept; area 1950.0 sq ft (181.16 m^2)

Fuselage and tail: length 147 ft 0 in (44.81 m); height 34 ft 10 in (10.62 m); tailplane span 44 ft 10 in (13.67 m); wheel base 57 ft 6 in (17.53 m)

Powerplant: four General Electric F101-GE-102s each rated at 14,600 lb (64.94 kN) dry and 30,780 lb (136.92 kN) afterburning thrusts

Weights: empty equipped 192,000 lb (87,091 kg); maximum take-off 477,000 lb (216,367 kg)

Fuel and load: internal fuel 195,000 lb (88,452 kg); maximum ordnance 75,000 lb (34,020 kg) carried internally and 59,000 lb (26,762 kg) carried externally

Speed: maximum level speed 'clean' at high altitude approximately 825 mph (1328 km/h); penetration speed at about 200 ft (61 m) in excess of 600 mph (965 km/h)

Range: maximum range on internal fuel 7455 miles (12,000 km)

Performance: service ceiling more than 50,000 ft (15,240 m)

BOEING KC-135R

Wing: span 130 ft 10 in (39.88 m); area 2433.0 sq ft (226.03 m^2)

Fuselage and tail: length 136 ft 3 in (41.53 m); height 41 ft 8 in (12.70 m); tailplane span 40 ft 3 in (12.27 m); wheel base 46 ft 7 in (14.20 m)

Powerplant: four CFM International F108-CF-100s each rated at 22,000 lb (97.86 kN) dry thrust

Weights: operating empty 106,303 lb (48,220 kg); maximum take-off 322,500 lb (146,284 kg)

Fuel and load: internal fuel 203,288 lb (92,212 kg)

Speed: maximum level speed at high altitude 610 mph (982 km/h); cruising speed at 35,000 ft (10,675 m) 532 mph (856 km/h)

Range: ferry range 9200 miles (14,806 km); radius to offload 150 per cent more fuel than KC-135A 2875 miles (4627 m)

BOEING E-3C SENTRY

Wing: span 145 ft 9 in (44.42 m); aspect ratio 7.0566; area 3050.0 sq ft (283.35 m^2)

Fuselage and tail: length 152 ft 11 in (46.61 m); height 41 ft 9 in (12.73 m); tailplane span 45 ft 9 in (13.95 m); wheel base 59 ft 0 in (17.98 m)

Powerplant: four Pratt & Whitney TF33-P-100/100As each rated at 21,000 lb (93.4 kN) dry thrust

Weights: operating empty 171,950 lb (77,996 kg); maximum take-off 325,000 lb (147,420 kg)

Fuel and load: internal 23,987 US gal (90,800 litres)

Speed: never-exceed speed Mach 0.95; maximum level speed at high altitude 530 mph (853 km/h)

Range: radius for a six-hour patrol without refuelling 1000 miles (1609 km); endurance without refuelling more than 11 hours

Performance: operating ceiling 29,000 ft (8840 m)

GRUMMAN EF-111A RAVEN

Wing: span 63 ft 0 in (19.20 m) spread and 31 ft 11.4 in (9.74 m) swept; area 525.0 sq ft (48.77m2) spread and 657.3 sq ft (61.07m^2) swept

Fuselage and tail: unit length 76 ft 0 in (23.16 m); height 20 ft 0 in (6.10 m)

Powerplant: two Pratt & Whitney TF30-P-3 each rated at 18,500 lb (82.29 kN) afterburning thrust

Weights: operating empty 55,275 lb (25,072 kg); normal take-off 70,000 lb (31,752 kg); maximum take-off 88,948 lb (4046 kg)

Fuel and load: internal fuel 32,493 lb (14,739 kg)

Speed: maximum speed at high altitude 1412 mph (2272 km/h); maximum combat speed 1377 mph (2216 km/h); average speed in combat area 584 mph (940 km/h)

Range: combat radius 929 miles (1495 km); unrefuelled endurance more than four hours

Performance: maximum rate of climb at sea level 3300 ft (1006 m) per minute; service ceiling 45,000 ft (13,715 m)

McDONNELL DOUGLAS F-15C EAGLE

Wing: span 42 ft 9.75 in (13.05 m); area 608.0 sq ft (56.48 m^2)

Fuselage and tail: length 63 ft 9 in (19.43 m); height 18 ft 5.5 in (5.63 m); tailplane span 28 ft 3 in (8.61 m); wheel base 17 ft 9.5 in (5.42 m)

Powerplant: two Pratt & Whitney F100-P-220s each rated at 14,370 lb (63.9 kN) dry and 23,450 lb (104.5 kN) afterburning thrusts, or two F100-P-229s each rated at 18,000 lb (81.1 kN) intermediate and 29,000 lb (129.0 kN) afterburning thrusts

Weights: operating empty 28,600 lb (12,793 kg); normal for interception mission 44,630 lb (20,244 kg); maximum take-off with FAST packs 68,000 lb (30,844 kg)

Fuel and load: internal fuel 13,455 lb (6103 kg); external fuel up to 9750 lb (4423 kg) in two FAST packs and 11,895 lb (5395 kg) in three 600-US gal (2271-litre) drop tanks; maximum ordnance 16,000 or 23,600 lb (7257 or 10,705 kg) with or without FAST packs

Speed: maximum level speed 'clean' at 36,000 ft (10,975 m) more than 1650 mph (2655 km/h); cruising speed 570 mph (917 km/h)

Range: ferry range with drop-tanks more than 2878 or 3450 miles (4631 or 5560 km) without or with FAST packs; interception combat radius 1222 miles (1967 km)

Performance: maximum rate of climb at sea level more than 50,000 ft (15,240 m) per minute; service ceiling 60,000 ft (18,290 m); absolute ceiling 100,000 ft (30,480 m); take-off distance 900 ft (274 m) on an interception mission; landing distance 3500 ft (1067 m) without a braking parachute

McDONNELL DOUGLAS F-15E (STRIKE EAGLE)

Wing: span 42 ft 9.75 in (13.05 m); area 608.0 sq ft (56.48m^2)

Fuselage and tail: length 63 ft 9 in (19.43 m); height 18 ft 5.5 in (5.63 m); tailplane span 28 ft 3 in (8.61 m); wheel base 17 ft 9.5 in (5.42 m)

Powerplant: two Pratt & Whitney F100-P-220s each rated at 14,370 lb (63.9 kN) dry and 23,450 lb (104.5 kN) afterburning thrusts

Weights: basic operating empty 31,700 lb (14,379 kg); maximum take-off 81,000 lb (36,741 kg)

Fuel and load: internal fuel 13,123 lb (5952 kg); external fuel 21,645 lb (9818 kg) in two FAST packs and up to three 610 US-gal (2309-litre) drop tanks; maximum ordnance 23,500 lb (10,659 kg)

Speed: maximum level speed 'clean' at high altitude more than 1650 mph (2655 km/h); cruising speed 570 mph (917 km/h)

Range: ferry range 3570 miles (5745 km) with FAST packs and drop tanks, and 2878 miles (4631 km) with drop tanks

Performance: maximum rate of climb at sea level more than 50,000 ft (15,240 m) per minute; service ceiling 60,000 ft (18,290 m); landing distance 3500 ft (1067 m) without a braking parachute

LOCKHEED F-16C FIGHTING FALCON

Wing: span over wingtip missile launchers 31 ft 0 in (9.45 m) and over wingtip missiles 32 ft 9.75 in (10.00 m); aspect ratio 3.0; area 300,0 sq ft (28.87 m^2)

Fuselage and tail: length 49 ft 4 in (15.03 m); height 16 ft 8.5 in (5.09 m); tailplane span 18 ft 3.75 in (5.58 m); wheel base 13 ft 1.5 in (4.00 m)

Powerplant: one Pratt & Whitney F100-P-220 rated at 14,370 lb (63.9 kN) dry and 23,450 lb (104.31 kN) afterburning thrust

Weights: empty 19,100 lb (8663 kg) with F110 turbofan; typical combat take-off 21,585 (9790 kg); maximum take-off 25,971 lb (11.372 kg) for an air-to-air mission without drop tanks, or 42,300 lb (19,187 kg) with maximum external load

Fuel and load: internal fuel 6972 lb (3162 kg); external fuel up to 6760 lb (3066 kg) in three 300-, 370-, 450- and 600-US-gal (1136-, 1400-, 1703- or 2271-litre) drop tanks; maximum ordnance 20,450 lb (9276 kg) for 5-g manoeuvre limit or 11,950 lb (5240 kg) for 9-g manoeuvre limit

Speed: maximum level speed 'clean' at 40,000 ft (12,190 m) more than 1320 mph (2124 km/h); maximum speed at sea level 915 mph (1472 km/h)

Range: ferry range more than 2415 miles (3890 km); combat radius on a hi-lo-hi mission with six 1000-lb (454-kg) bombs 340 miles (547 km)

Performance: maximum rate of climb at sea level more than 50,000 ft (15,240 m) per minute; service ceiling more than 50,000 ft (15,240 m); typical take-off distance 2500 ft (762 m); typical landing distance 2500 ft (762 m)